Prayers

FOR A SMALL CHILD

Illustrated by
ELOISE WILKIN

Random House  New York

Copyright © 1984 by Random House, Inc. All rights reserved under International and Pan-American Copyright Conventions. Published in the United States by Random House, Inc., New York, and simultaneously in Canada by Random House of Canada Limited, Toronto.

Library of Congress Cataloging in Publication Data: Main entry under title: Prayers for a small child. SUMMARY: Prayers of petition, praise, and thanksgiving for the things common to a child's life. 1. Children—Prayer-books and devotions—English. [1. Prayers] I. Wilkin, Eloise Burns. BV4870.P65 1984 242'.82 83-16050 ISBN: 0-394-86281-3 (trade): 0-394-96281-8 (lib. bdg.)

Manufactured in the United States of America 3 4 5 6 7 8 9 0

Now, before I run to play,
    Let me not forget to pray
To God, who kept me through the night
    And waked me with the morning light.

Help me, Lord, love Thee more
    Than I ever loved before,
In my work and in my play,
    Be Thou with me through the day.

Thank you for the world so sweet,
Thank you for the food we eat.
Thank you for the birds that sing,
Thank you, God, for everything.

God, our Father, kind and good,
We thank Thee for our daily food,
We thank Thee for our families dear,
We thank Thee for Thy love and care.

God is great, and God is good,
And we thank Him for our food,
By His hand we all are fed;
Thank you, Lord, for our daily bread.

God made the little fishes,
  The tadpoles and the frogs,
The spiders and the beetles
  We find beneath the logs.
He made the beasties, big and small,
  And he loves them, one and all.

Winter's gone, and bright warm sun
Tells us springtime has begun;
For budding flower and busy bee,
Dear God, we give our thanks to Thee.

Thank God, who sends the gentle rain
That thirsty flowers may drink again—
For puddles on the garden path
Where little birds may take a bath.

Give us, Father, every day
Work to do and time for play;
Help us to be kind and good,
To act like Thy children should.

For summer, winter, spring, and fall,
For your watch-care over all,
For the rainbow's promise true,
We give our thanks, dear God, to you.

God made the sun
And God made the tree,
God made the mountains
And God made me.

Thank you for each happy day,
For fun, for friends,
And work and play;
Thank you for your loving care,
Here at home and everywhere.

When winter is here
A cold wind blows.
My fingers are cold
And so are my toes.
But down by the fire
I'm warm as can be.
Thank God for the fire,
So cozy to see.

All things bright and beautiful,
   All creatures, great and small,
All things wise and wonderful,
   The Lord God made them all.

*   *   *

He gave us eyes to see them,
    And lips that we might tell
How great is God Almighty,
    Who has made all things well!

A gentle prayer is what I'll say
To close this peaceful, gentle day.

With gratitude that I have heard
The pre-dawn chirpings of a bird.

With thankfulness that I have seen
The many hues of summer-green.

With singing heart that I could feel
The soft warm grasses when I kneel.

With love for those who give me care
I softly close my gentle prayer.

I see the moon,
And the moon sees me;
God bless the moon,
And God bless me.

Father, unto You I pray,
You have guarded me all day;
Safe I am while in your sight,
Safely let me sleep tonight.

Bless my friends, the whole world bless;
Help me to learn helpfulness;
Keep me ever in Your sight;
So to all I say good night.

Good night! Good night!
Far flies the light;
But still God's love
Shall flame above,
Making all bright.
Good night! Good night!

Now I lay me down to sleep,
I pray Thee, Lord, Thy child to keep:
Thy love guard me through the night
And wake me with the morning light.

The Lord's Prayer

Our Father who art in heaven,
Hallowed be Thy name.
Thy kingdom come;
Thy will be done
on earth as it is in heaven.
Give us this day our daily bread,
And forgive us our trespasses,
As we forgive those who trespass against us.
And lead us not into temptation,
But deliver us from evil:
For Thine is the kingdom,
And the power, and the glory,
For ever. Amen.